From Pressure to Praise

Stress Strategies From God's Word

From Pressure to Praise

Stress Strategies From God's Word

by
Robyn Gool

CONQUERORS
PUBLISHING

Unless otherwise indicated,
all Scripture quotations are taken from
the *King James Version* of the Bible.

Scripture quotations marked AMP are taken from *The Amplified Bible, New Testament.* Copyright © 1958, 1987 by The Lockman Foundation, La Habra, California.

From Pressure to Praise —
Stress Strategies From God's Word
ISBN 978-0-9648460-8-1
Copyright © 1992 by Robyn Gool, Reprinted 2007
P. O. Box 240433
Charlotte, North Carolina 28224

Published by Conquerors Publishing
7228 Old Pineville Road
Charlotte, North Carolina 28217

Contents

From Pressure to Praise

Stress Strategies From God's Word

1

Everyone Deals With Pressure

Pressure is no respecter of persons or of age or nationality. Everybody has to deal with it at some point, even children.

There is pressure on husbands to be better husbands, pressure on wives to be better wives, pressure on children to be better children and pressure on students to be better students.

A child who has had a good semester may come home from school with grades of A's and B's and maybe one C. Too many times the parents overlook the A's and B's and react to that one C, pressuring the child: "You should do better! What is this C doing on your report card?"

Children, particularly teenagers, feel peer pressure. They want to serve Jesus. They want to live right. They want to respect their parents and honor their parents' moral codes. But if these teenagers are living a Christian life, their friends call them "square," "old-fashioned" or "out of it." Their friends pressure them, asking, "Why aren't you smoking, drinking and partying with us?"

On their jobs, people deal with the pressure of trying to keep up with their co-workers. Maybe someone's co-worker produces more than he does, and the person has to try to work a little harder to produce more.

The Battle
Is in the Mind

Many times when people are faced with pressure, their minds begin to run wild; their thoughts press in on them. They throw up their hands and run. They escape. They turn to drugs or alcohol, partying or illicit sex. Or they turn to television and sit in front of it for hours. But they will not find the answer they need watching television unless there is a man of God on, preaching the Word.

They are hoping that if they just run long enough, the problems will vanish and the pressure will disappear. But when they stop running, the problems are still there. Problems and pressure do not just vanish; they have to be dealt with. And God's Word gives us the solution to dealing with pressure.

> **Wherefore seeing we also are compassed about with so great a cloud of witnesses, let us lay aside every weight, and the sin which doth so easily beset us, and let us run with patience the race that is set before us, looking unto Jesus the author and finisher of our faith; who for the joy that was set before him endured the cross, despising the shame, and is set down at the right hand of the throne of God.**

> **For consider him** (Jesus) **that endured such contradiction of sinners against himself, lest ye be wearied and faint in your minds. Ye have not yet resisted unto blood, striving against sin.**
>
> **Hebrews 12:1-4**

Verse 3 tells us to **consider him** (Jesus) **. . . lest ye be wearied and faint in your minds.** Pressure comes against the mind — it is all in the mind. That is where it all starts — where the battle is — you will either win or lose, depending upon how you deal with your mind. If you faint in your mind, you have already lost.

The Word says, through Peter, that we are to follow Jesus and walk in His steps. (1 Peter 2:21) When you are faced with pressure, the first thing you need to do is consider Jesus. You cannot look at your problems, your circumstances or the pressure; you have to look at Jesus. Otherwise you will get weary and faint.

Through Hebrews 12:1-4 written by the Apostle Paul, the Holy Spirit is telling us to consider Jesus, because Jesus, our example, had to face pressure, and He faced it properly. He overcame it.

Jesus Faced Pressure

> **And he came out, and went, as he was wont, to the mount of Olives; and his disciples also followed him. And when he was at the place, he said unto them, Pray that ye enter not into temptation.**
>
> **And he was withdrawn from them about a stone's cast, and kneeled down, and prayed, saying, Father, if thou be willing, remove this cup from me: nevertheless not my will, but thine, be done.**
>
> **And there appeared an angel unto him from heaven, strengthening him. And being in an agony**

**he prayed more earnestly: and his sweat was as it were
great drops of blood falling down to the ground.**

   **And when he rose up from prayer, and was come
to his disciples, he found them sleeping for sorrow,
and said unto them, Why sleep ye? rise and pray, lest
ye enter into temptation.**

Luke 22:39-46

In the flesh, Jesus did not want to go to Calvary.
His flesh was saying, "You don't want those spikes
going into Your wrists. You don't want those spikes
going into Your feet. You don't want a spear in Your
side."

But Jesus' Spirit was saying, "It's the only way
for man to get back in right standing with God!" (Matt.
26:41 says that the spirit is willing, but the flesh is
weak.)

Then the flesh would say, "No, you don't want
that! You want to live!"

That pressure against Jesus mounted until it was
so great that Jesus fell to His knees and cried out,
"Father, if there is any way, let this cup pass!"

Jesus dealt with the type of pressure that you and
I will never have to experience. In the Garden of
Gethsemane, pressure came against Him to such an
extreme, His sweat was as great drops of blood.

Consider Jesus

You and I have never had pressure coming against
us to the point of our sweat being as blood. When
problems come our way — storms, tribulations, hard
times and crises — and we say, "How can I get out
of this? How can I deal with this?" we can consider
Jesus. We need to turn to Jesus. He has dealt with

pressure far worse than any we have faced. We need to look at God's Word. Looking at Jesus keeps us on target and keeps us going. Jesus strengthens us. He encourages, motivates and challenges us.

As believers, we need to know how to deal with pressure in order to accurately represent the Lord Jesus. Jesus is a winner, and He expects us to be winners. He expects us to represent Him in the same way on earth He represented His heavenly Father. In order for us to do that, we must know how to be winners over pressure.

In this book, we consider Jesus. We look at what God's Word says about dealing with pressure because God's Word is our answer.

2

Think in Line
With God's Word

Many people "choke" under pressure. Athletes know how that works.

A basketball player is at the line; he has the opportunity to win the game with a free throw. He's got the ball, the score is tied, and time has run out. He was fouled right before the buzzer went off and has the opportunity to win the game without going into overtime.

He steps to the line. He bounces the ball. He looks at the basket and bounces again. Something is happening here! It's called "choking."

He sees the camera. His mind says, "You make this basket, man, and you're on the front page tomorrow!" He sees his little girlfriend over on the sidelines.

Then his mind says, "But if you miss . . . ."

He tightens up. He gets the ball; he lets it go. And it hits — nothing! He misses! It's an air ball.

The guys say, *"He choked!"*

He choked under the pressure. In everyday practice — when the situation wasn't pressurized — he had made that same shot a hundred times. But he had the only opportunity to win the game without going into overtime, and he choked. The pressure got to him. It was too much for him.

A lot of people choke under pressure. They get wearied and faint in their minds. If we faint in our minds we can't win because the Bible says, **Let us not be weary in well doing:** *for in due season we shall reap, if we faint not* (Gal. 6:9).

Let's look at the word, "if." "If" means there is a condition. That means *we* have to do something in order to receive the reward. What we have to do is take control of our minds. Remember that you win or lose depending upon how you deal with the thoughts that come to mind.

No matter how close the game is — the game of life I mean now — no matter how tight the score is, Christians have no business choking!

Greater Is He That Is in Us

Consider Jesus **lest ye be wearied and faint in your minds.** Greater is He that is in us, than he that is in the world. (1 John 4:4) The same Spirit that raised Jesus from the dead dwells in us, and He will quicken our mortal bodies. (Rom. 8:11) We can do all things through Christ which strengthens us. (Phil. 4:13) We don't have to choke!

As we saw before, for Jesus the pressure was so great that He fell to His knees and asked the Father to let the cup of the crucifixion pass from Him. But He overcame that pressure. His spirit man said, **Nevertheless not my will, but thine, be done** (Luke 22:42).

Cast Down Imaginations

For though we walk in the flesh, we do not war after the flesh: (For the weapons of our warfare are not carnal, but mighty through God to the pulling down of strong holds;)

Casting down imaginations, and every high thing that exalteth itself against the knowledge of God, and bringing into captivity every thought to the obedience of Christ.

2 Corinthians 10:3-5

To not faint in our minds, we are to *cast down* imaginations (or **reasonings** — AMP). The devil will try to reason us out of acting on God's Word or try to keep us from acting on it by putting all types of thoughts into our minds. The Bible says to cast down those imaginations, because the "faith fight" is in the mind.

If we can keep the bad thoughts that come to our minds from staying there, then we can win, because we act on or respond to only the thoughts we decide to allow within ourselves. We decide through our thinking processes to obey God's Word. So if we think in line with God's Word, what we decide will be based on God's Word, and we'll walk in line with it. We'll win!

That's why we win or lose depending on how we handle the thoughts that come to mind. We must make sure that we cast down every reasoning, every thought, every thought process or pattern inconsistent with the Word of God that comes into our minds.

If we don't cast down those imaginations, before long we will be thinking so much about the way things look that we will just reason ourselves right out of God's way of looking at things.

A Wrong Thought
Is Not a Sin

Some people think, *If I'm already thinking something wrong, I might as well say it* or *If I think something that is wrong, I'm sinning.* That isn't true!

If the moment a bad thought comes into our minds, and we choose not to entertain it or dwell on it, but cast it down, then we haven't sinned.

If every bad thought that comes to our minds is automatically a sin, why would the Bible tell us about the importance of casting down imaginations? Second Corinthians 10:5 would not be in the Bible. But this verse *is* in the Bible to show us that we have the opportunity, the privilege, the responsibility and the obligation as believers to take authority over our thought life *so that we will not faint.*

If we faint, we can't receive from God. And if we're not receiving from God, we might as well go back to the ways of the world. By that I don't mean that we might as well forget about God. I mean that if we can't receive from God, we're just like an unbeliever for all *practical* purposes.

The reason God wants us to receive Jesus — His only begotten Son Who was sent into the world to save us — is *not* so that we can just hold on until the end and live like beggars down here until one day we get the pie in the sky in heaven.

If that were true, I would say:

"If that's what the Christian life is all about, I might as well not serve Jesus. If I can't have a God Who can turn my life around down here, then why should I serve Him?

"Lord, I want answers! I don't want it all when I get to heaven. I'm down here now, Lord! What do You have for me down here? Can You heal my body now? Can You turn my finances around?"

The answer is, *yes!*

"Well, do it, God! I want it now!"

If I have to wait until I get to heaven, I might as well try to wait until I'm on my death bed to say, 'Jesus, come into my life.' Then I could go right to heaven and get whatever is up there. If I've got to live down and out, defeated and discouraged like a beggar down here, why should I serve Him?

Of course, not everybody down here is down and out. There are gangsters, pimps and drug dealers walking around in nice clothes and driving nice cars. I might as well get over into that if that's the only way I'm going to be happy down here. Or I may as well become a workaholic, doing all I can to climb the corporate ladder to attain all the material things I can. I may lose my family on the way up (as many have), but at least I'll be able to pay my bills, live decently, and enjoy life to a certain degree.

But no! Praise God! No way!

My God is able! He is well able! (Eph. 3:20) Jesus said, **I am come that they might have life, and that they might have it more abundantly** (John 10:10), and

He was talking about life right here on earth. I can receive that abundant life right now!

I can begin to get into God's Word and find out what He has supplied for me. I can begin to get that Word into my heart, begin to speak it forth out of my mouth and begin to walk in it every day of my life. I'll begin to see manifesting in my life all the provisions of my Almighty God — prosperity, health, peace of mind, fine clothes, a better job, a better home. Then when I get to heaven, I get my mansion.

Serving Jesus benefits us down here as well as when we get to heaven. There is no better life to live than a life for Jesus. The riches of this world will pass away. But God's riches are eternal.

Worldly Reasonings
Can Be an Idol

You see, God says one thing about a situation and the world usually says something else. God says, "I'll meet all of your needs according to My riches in glory by Christ Jesus" (Phil. 4:19), but the world says, "No way! You don't have enough. How is God going to work that out? Just look at your bank book. Look at how much money you make every couple weeks. There's no way. You had better borrow from your grandmother. You had better pawn something or sell something."

Those are reasonings. The Bible tells you to cast down those reasonings (imaginations). If you don't, you'll grow weary and faint. You'll faint in your mind. Those bad thoughts are going to come — thoughts that tell you that God isn't going to come through for you, the situation is impossible, you're going to lose your car — and right then, you've got a choice to make. You can either entertain those thoughts and allow them to put more pressure on you, or you can cast them down, because those thoughts and that logic are exalting themselves against God.

If you allow those thoughts to be exalted above God, you have just made an idol. Worldly reasoning has become an idol. It has taken the place of the Word of our heavenly Father. Therefore, we have to cast it down.

How do we cast it down?

We simply say:

"I'm not going to think on that. I'm not going to entertain that, in the name of Jesus. It does not match up with God's Word; therefore, I put it down right now. I will not allow my mind to think on it or dwell on it. I will continue to look upon God's Word which says that my God supplies all of my needs, *all* of them, according to His riches in glory by Christ Jesus! I cast down all imaginations."

Think God's Thoughts

So when we cast down those wrong thoughts — those evil thoughts — we shouldn't just leave our minds idle.

Philippians 4:8 tells us:

> **Finally, brethren, whatsoever things are true, whatsoever things are honest, whatsoever things are just, whatsoever things are pure, whatsoever things are lovely, whatsoever things are of good report; if there be any virtue, and if there be any praise, think on these things.**

Replace those wrong thoughts with good thoughts. Isaiah 26:3 says, ''I (God) will keep you in perfect peace if your mind is stayed on Me, because you trust in Me.'' (That's my version.)

The way to keep your mind on God is by the Word of God. Meditate on it day and night. (Josh. 1:8) That's how you deal with your thought life. As you keep the Word of God flowing in your mind, in your thinking processes, you're considering Jesus. You're dealing with pressure.

Consider Jesus lest you grow weary and faint in your minds. If you don't get weary in well doing and don't faint, you will reap. As a child of God, you can win over every problem that comes your way.

Say to yourself:

''I make up my mind right now to win! I'll cast down those imaginations and replace them with God's thoughts. I'll never choke — no matter how tough it is. I consider Jesus. I don't have to choke under pressure!''

3

Take Time To Act — Not React

Let the life of Jesus be the example.

John 8:1-6 says:

> Jesus went unto the mount of Olives. And early in the morning he came again into the temple, and all the people came unto him; and he sat down, and taught them.
>
> And the scribes and Pharisees brought unto him a woman taken in adultery; and when they had set her in the midst, they say unto him, Master, this woman was taken in adultery, in the very act. Now Moses in the law commanded us, that such should be stoned: but what sayest thou?
>
> This they said, tempting him, that they might have to accuse him. But Jesus stooped down, and with his finger wrote on the ground, as though he heard them not.

Early in the morning, Jesus went into the temple. All the people came to Him, and He sat down and began to teach them the Word of God. Among those people were scribes and Pharisees — religious folks. By "religious" I mean having a form of godliness but denying the power thereof (2 Tim. 3:5); living by the letter of the law with no love, mercy or compassion; having an air of right standing with God because of works and no relationship whatsoever. (It's sad to be religious! But it makes you glad that you're a Christian — that you have a relationship with Jesus, instead of just living according to a set of rules. Just being religious won't do anything for you. But being a Christian will change you, your life, your circumstances.)

Here came the scribes and the Pharisees dragging this woman along. Everyone stopped, looked around, and there were these religious men. Supposedly, they were the leaders responsible for guiding the people to God. Everybody stopped. Jesus stopped. The Pharisees threw the woman down at the feet of Jesus.

"Jesus, we've caught this woman in adultery! We've caught her in the very act!"

Remember — it was early in the morning. To have caught her in the act means the religious leaders had to have stayed up all night, going around the village, looking in this hut, looking in that hut, just like Peeping Toms. It's sad to say, but there are some people who love to find dirt in other peoples' lives. That's not what Jesus is all about.

Religious people like to find out things that are wrong in other peoples' lives. They like to criticize. They like to gossip and tell things that are bad. But people who are born again should be longsuffering. They're patient. They realize that they aren't perfect themselves. Out of love they reach down and pick up that brother or that sister.

But these religious men dragged that woman in and threw her down at the feet of Jesus. They had probably been searching all night throughout the village for someone to catch in the act. The law called for her to be stoned.

"What do You say, Jesus?"

Here we are, talking about dealing with pressure. And I don't know about you, but I can see how this situation put the pressure on Jesus. It seems evident to me that here was pressure presenting itself to Jesus, and He had to deal with it right there on the spot.

All of us have to deal with pressure at some point in time, and it comes in all different ways, in all different packages and in all shapes. Pressure has all different styles, and we have to deal with it as believers.

In this case, Jesus knew what the Word of God said. The law said that any woman taken or caught in adultery must be stoned. Jesus knew that. That's pressure. Jesus must have been thinking, *What am I going to do? Am I going to side with these religious people and stone this woman?*

The Bible says He *stooped down* and, with His finger, wrote something on the ground. I wonder why? I believe He did that because He had to get Himself together. Remember — Jesus was a man. Many people forget that. They think He was just divine.

He became a man. He left all of His divine attributes and power and became a man born of the virgin Mary. Jesus' blood was pure blood. He walked the earth as a man under the Old Covenant, never relying on anything that He had before He became a man, but only on what every man had available to him — the Word of God.

He relied on that covenant. He walked in that covenant. He was a man when this pressure situation presented itself to Him. He stooped down. He wrote on the ground.

I don't really think He was writing in the sense of *really* writing. He was just scribbling. You know how we do sometimes. We just get a piece of paper and begin to doodle. Our minds are wandering. I imagine that's what Jesus was doing. He was just thinking, getting Himself together, making sure that He gave the right answer, making sure that He didn't move on impulse or just react.

John 8:6 says, **But Jesus stooped down, and with his finger wrote on the ground, as though he heard them not.** He knew He had to deal with this situation properly. The Pharisees were applying pressure. They just kept pressing Him and pressing Him: ''What do You say, Jesus? What do You say? What do You say . . . .?''

Verses 7,8:

> So when they *continued* asking him, he lifted up himself, and said unto them, He that is without sin among you, let him first cast a stone at her. And again he stooped down, and wrote on the ground.

Sounds like a good answer to me!

Verses 9-11:

> And they which heard it, being convicted by their own conscience, went out one by one, beginning at

the eldest, even unto the last: and Jesus was left alone,
and the woman standing in the midst.

When Jesus lifted up himself, and saw none but
the woman, he said unto her, Woman, where are those
thine accusers? hath no man condemned thee? She
said, No man, Lord. And Jesus said unto her, Neither
do I condemn thee: go, and sin no more.

Evaluate the Situation

Jesus took His time. He got Himself together.
When the pressure came at Him, He took time to
answer correctly.

And that's the problem where many people are
concerned. When the pressure hits, what they do is
react. They move out on the first thing that comes into
their mind. They don't take time to evaluate the
situation. They don't take time to be still and know that
He is God. (Ps. 46:10) They just panic. Then they react
out of that.

Jesus could have panicked, but He didn't.

Consider Jesus.

The first thing we have to do in order to deal with
pressure is to take the time to be still and know that
He is God. We have to take the time to evaluate the
situation. Don't just react. Don't move on impulse.
Don't just jump after the first thing that comes into
your mind or at the first escape route. Many times
that's what people do. The first thing that comes into
their mind is, ''Oh, but I can get money from Aunt
So-and-So.''

But that's not what Jesus did! He didn't jump after
the first thing that presented itself.

He took time. He stooped down and scribbled, just thinking. He made sure He didn't utter the first words that came to His mind.

James 1:19 says, **Be slow to speak.** That's the first thing you have to do to deal with pressure correctly. When you're looking at pressure head on, be still and know that the Lord is God. Look at the situation and then go in your prayer closet. Find out what the Word has to say.

Frequently you're faced with all kinds of pressure on the job. Just be still. Don't say anything. Allow the Holy Spirit time to give you the right answer. Just shut your mind down and begin to pray in the Spirit under your breath, silently, to yourself, within yourself. Allow the Holy Spirit to begin to formulate the right answer within you.

I believe that's what Jesus was doing. He was just allowing the Holy Spirit to use the Word of God that He had in His Spirit, because Jesus was a very studious individual. The Bible says, **Jesus increased in wisdom and stature, and in favour with God and man** (Luke 2:52). That verse means He studied the Word of God. He took the time to allow His purpose for being on earth to come to the forefront, to come to His thinking. Then He stood up.

After He received the wisdom of God out of His inner man, He said, **He that is without sin among you let him first cast a stone at her** (John 8:7).

Be Slow To Speak

Wherefore, my beloved brethren, let every man be swift to hear, slow to speak, slow to wrath.
James 1:19

28

Many Christians have turned this Scripture around. They've been swift to speak and slow to hear. That isn't what the Word says. Consider Jesus. He was slow to speak when faced with pressure. At the time of pressure, He didn't say anything. He was silent. He was still.

As James 1:19 says, **Be slow to speak.**

I wonder why? Well, the answer is simple — so that the Holy Spirit can provide the right words to say.

The Bible says, **Trust in the Lord with all thine heart; and lean not unto thine own understanding. In all thy ways acknowledge him, and he shall direct thy paths** (Prov. 3:5,6).

I believe Jesus stooped down, acknowledging His Father: "Father, what's Your mind? What's Your plan? What's Your will here? What's Your idea?"

And that's what we must do. Consider Jesus. What did He do?

"Haste Makes Waste"

There's a saying, "Haste makes waste." There's truth to that. I've found that plenty of times when I'm moving in a hurry, I just wind up having to go back and do everything over again.

When I was growing up, my mom and dad would say, "Now it's your turn to mop the floor." I just wanted to get the thing over with. We were brought up mopping on our knees. Today we have it easy. We have mops that enable us to just lean over and squeeze the rollers out. But my mom and dad said, "You get down on your knees and get it clean!"

I didn't always want to get down there. If a program was coming on television that I wanted to see, I would just hurry up and go do the mopping and call it done. "Mama, I'm finished!"

I didn't know she was going to say, "I'm going to go see what he did."

She would go in there and start checking places that I didn't think she was going to check. Then she would say, "Get back in this kitchen!" And I had to do the whole thing over again. I learned how *haste makes waste*. Hurrying didn't do me any good, because I had to go right back and do it all over again. It always pays to do it right the first time. And when it comes to pressure, the right way is to be still and know that the Lord is God. Take the time to see the total picture. Then do it right.

Impulse Can Equal Pressure

A lady may get her husband angry with her when she goes to the mall and — after her husband has already told her he only wants her to spend a certain amount — she buys according to impulse. That puts its own kind of pressure on a marriage.

Her husband has already looked at the budget. He knows how much is coming in, how much is going out and how much he has on hand. He knows how much he wants her to spend. She says, "Okay, dear," then heads for the mall. She has her mind made up to be obedient and follow the flow of her husband and the budget. But then, all of a sudden, she's on her way to a certain shop and suddenly something says, "Look at that store!" It's a shoe store. She isn't shopping for shoes. She says, "I didn't come for shoes."

Then something says, "But you need some shoes."

So she counters with, "But I didn't come for shoes; I came for a dress."

And something says, "But it's a sale."

Then she says, "I've only got a certain amount of money to spend."

And then there's that "something" again: "You can make him a cake. He'll forgive you."

So there she goes. Shoe sale, shoe sale! She spends the extra money. And instead of stopping at shoes and saying, "I won't buy the dress," she says, "I'm going to get the dress *now*!"

And she comes home with both.

She couldn't deal with the pressure. And now she has a new kind of pressure to deal with when her husband says, "Wait a minute, baby — what's the deal?"

The simple truth is this: she acted on impulse.

The enemy has used that same kind of pressure to destroy marriages — to spend more money than what has been allotted.

When a lady is out there in the mall and knows she's on a tight budget, when she knows she's out there to buy a specific thing, she needs to keep her eyes looking straight ahead.

Turn not to the left or to the right. Go straight to that store! That's what the Bible tells us to do. (Prov. 4:27) Then if she glances over and happens to see a sale, how does she deal with that pressure? She should consider Jesus.

What did He do? He took time to be still. He did not act on impulse. When she sees that sale, she needs to be still. Be still!

She needs to remind herself, "What am I here for? What's our budget? My husband is the head of the home. Let me flow with him."

Sometimes men overspend on impulse, too. With men, most times it's a more expensive item — a VCR, a car, a personal computer, etc. They are like little boys that have to buy the new toy on the market. Only this toy breaks the budget. It's a status fulfillment — an insecurity. It's trouble. But whoever it is needs to remember to consider Jesus. Be still. Know that the Lord is God. Then deal with that impulse!

Let the Holy Spirit Give You an Answer

Remember what James said: **Be slow to speak.**

Allow the Holy Spirit to bring to your mind what you need to say. In Colossians 4:6, the Bible says, **Let your speech be always with grace, seasoned with salt, that ye may know how ye ought to answer every man.**

The way this Scripture can become a reality in our lives is if we are also slow to speak.

Too many people are quick on their feet. I don't want to have the reputation of being quick on my feet. In other words, the person who is quick on his feet always has a quick answer for everything. I want to be slow to speak. I want to allow the Holy Spirit an opportunity to give me the answer. Be slow to move, slow to respond.

Let every man be swift to hear, slow to speak . . . .
James 1:19

Jesus was slow to speak. The reason we as Christians need to be slow to speak is so that we can allow the Holy Spirit an opportunity to bring the right answer to our thinking processes.

The man who's quick on his feet always has an answer for everything no matter what situation he's in, no matter when you catch him. If you shoot some questions at him, he always has a quick answer. He thinks sharply, quickly. He moves out on impulse much of the time.

I don't want to be known as that type of individual. I know that if I don't take time to think through a situation, to evaluate questions, to really analyze what is being asked, then I'll say something that may not make any sense. I want to be slow to speak. I want to make sure I'm giving sound counsel. I don't want to be saying something just to be saying something, even if it may sound good or scriptural. I don't need a reputation.

Jesus is the One Who ought to be exalted. He is the One to be glorified. Not me. All I want to do is share Jesus, and I want to share Him accurately.

Slowing down and seeking the counsel of the Holy Spirit will help you say things that will exalt Jesus, and it will also help to keep you from acting on impulse, whether that is buying on impulse or speaking the first thing that comes to your mind. Act on James 1:19 and Colossians 4:6. You can avoid the extra pressure that comes with being impulsive.

God wants us to give sound counsel. He wants us to have sound wisdom. He wants us to give the right answer in every situation to every human being. **Let your speech be always with grace, seasoned with salt, that ye may know how ye ought to answer every man.** (Coloss. 4:6)

In order to do that, sometimes we have to be still, know that He is God, trust in Him with all our heart and lean not to our own understanding.

Consider Jesus. When you consider Him, you realize that the pressure for Him became so great, His sweat was as drops of blood falling from His forehead. And He still overcame that pressure. Therefore, no matter what you're going through, if you just look to Jesus, you can say, "Jesus made it, and His pressure was far greater than mine, so I can make it, because I have Jesus on the inside of me. **I can do all things through Christ which strengtheneth me.**" (Phil. 4:13)

Then never move in a hurry; never make a quick decision. Evaluate the situation. Be still and know He is God. And allow the Holy Spirit to give you the answer.

4

Take Time
To Make Decisions

Sometimes salesmen pressure you. They may not mean to do it. They're just trying to sell their product. They have to make a living. But no matter how cordial they try to be, no matter how polite they are, no matter how patient they try to be, they can really put on the pressure.

We have to know how to deal with that. You deal with it by making up your mind to never make a quick decision or a hasty one no matter how bad the pressure gets. If you don't have the Holy Spirit directing you to go ahead and decide right there on the spot, then don't make a decision on the spot. Wait. Be slow to move. Say, "I need time to evaluate this. I need time to think about this. I have to go back and look at my budget to see if I can afford this."

At that moment, on the spot, it all sounds good. It looks so good. It seems like you just can't do without it.

Sometimes we just move on that impulse. Then afterwards we say, "I forgot about my car payment. I forgot about my house payment. I forgot about my child's tuition. I forgot to buy the clothing I need for this trip or project." Finally, you say, "I can't afford this." But it's too late. You have allowed the pressure to move you, only to discover that "all that glitters is not gold."

I remember one time my wife and I received a letter from a camping facility. The owners sold parcels of land on the campground. In the letter they said, "Just come and visit. Check us out. No pressure involved! And for your coming, we'll give you one of these prizes . . . ." The prizes looked good — a television, a camera, a vacation trip to Florida or Las Vegas.

A few days after we got the letter, we got a phone call from the people who sent it, asking if their letter had arrived. Marilyn, my wife, basically did the talking. When I realized that she was talking to a representative of this company, I said, "Baby — wait a minute!" She put her hand over the phone.

I said, "I don't want to go. Tell him no!"

She said, "But I want to go! I want to go!"

I said, "I don't want to go. Tell him no!"

The man was still on the line. She was still holding her hand over the receiver saying, "I want to go! It'll be a nice drive."

Finally, I said we would go. So she told him we would come and what day.

When we got there, we had to wait in a reception area. They had coffee, soda and refreshments for us while we were waiting. After a long time, the representative came out and said, "Oh, you're Mr. and Mrs. Gool?" We introduced ourselves.

He gave us a tour and drove us around the grounds. He said we could have this and that and pointed out how beautiful a place it was. While he was saying all of this, I said, "Let me ask you a question. Do I have to decide today?" He stopped and said, "Oh no, you don't have to decide today. But it's a nice place, and you can bring your children."

I said, "Listen — I'll tell you this right now. I'm not an outdoorsman; I'm not a camper. I've really never gotten into camping, but I like this facility. I like this campground, and I've got friends I could bring with me if I bought a piece of land here. I've got a lot of friends who love to fish and camp and different things like that. But do I have to decide today?"

He said, "No — you don't have to decide today. There's no pressure involved in this at all."

"Good," I said.

Finally, he said, "Well, let's go and talk to my brother because he can explain things a little better and write up a contract if you like."

I said, "Sure, let's do that. But I don't plan to make a decision today."

This is *exactly* how it went.

I asked him at least four or five times if I had to make a decision that day. He told me repeatedly, "No — you don't have to decide today."

So we drove back to the main office. He went off to talk to his brother. I noticed that he was gone a long time. I told my wife, "It's probably one of those deals that if you don't decide today, you can't have this particular deal, this particular discount. Otherwise, it wouldn't take them this long."

"No Pressure Involved"

We sat there and sat there. Finally, he came out with his brother. His brother sat down with us. He said, "Mr. and Mrs. Gool, I understand that you like this area here."

I said, "Yes, we're very much interested in it, but do I have to decide today?"

He kept talking and said, "Let me explain something to you here." He went on to explain some things. He said, "You know, we can give you a good deal. Because we've just had about 20 or so people who bought a lot in this area, we can get you involved in the discount package that we gave them. You can actually buy a lot below the price we mentioned earlier."

I said, "But do I have to decide today?"

He said, "Well, let me go back a minute."

I told him, "If we have to decide today, it's no deal. I'm not going to do it."

They just kept putting on the pressure.

Finally, he said, "Well, I'm telling you, if you want this deal, you've got to make up your mind right now."

I said, "But your brother said . . . . "

"If you want this deal, you have to make up your mind right now," he repeated.

I said, "Well, good day, sir. We're not going to buy this. I need time to evaluate. I told your brother we're not going to make a decision on the spur of the moment, so we'll just say good day to you."

He got up and said, "Well . . . 'bye."

His brother stayed there and kept talking with us, trying to relay some things to us. The second brother came back as if to say, "Get rid of these people! They're not going to buy today!" Finally, the other brother just said, "Well, Mr. and Mrs. Gool, we're going to have to say goodbye to you."

I told my wife that these people send you a letter saying "no pressure involved" to get you to visit the facility. When you get there — no matter how many times you say you're not going to buy today — they keep trying to make it so attractive and tempting that you will decide that day. They just won't accept your "no" as an answer. They keep pushing their product.

The enemy is using this to put more pressure on you. You like the offer, you want it and you're listening to them constantly telling you, "This is the day you can get the best deal." More and more pressure builds up on you.

Many people allow that type of pressure to cause them to buy a house, a tract of land or an automobile when they weren't ready financially to do it. The salesman may have said that day was the last day on that particular deal, but I want you to know something:

That may be the last day at that place, but there are some more deals in other places.

Be slow to move in making decisions. Look at the overall picture. Don't blow your budget. Don't blow your finances because of high-pressure sales because something is so beautiful. If you were to buy it, you wouldn't even be able to enjoy it because you would have to get an extra job to pay for it. You would have to eat beans every night.

Let the Lord Bless You

Let Jesus bless you. The Bible says that if you delight yourself in the Lord, He will give you the desires of your heart. (Ps. 37:4.) Malachi 3:10 tells us that if you give ten percent of your income to your storehouse — if you tithe — God will open up the windows of heaven and pour you out a blessing that you won't be able to contain.

Just continue to do what God's Word says. Continue to honor your budget. Continue to walk within your means as you are applying the Word of God, and let God bless you. He'll promote you. He'll exalt you. *Just let God do it!*

We have to be bold enough to say "no" no matter how many times the salesmen call back. The answer is still "no!" Sometimes because they call us back a few times, we feel like we have to go ahead, succumb and buy. But no, the answer is still "no!"

Learn To Say ''No''

I've found that many Christians have problems saying ''no.'' Either they don't have the boldness, or they're just fearful of using it. They're afraid to say "no."

You have to say "no" if something is going to hurt you. Don't try to keep up with somebody else. Forget the Joneses; they may go bankrupt. Let God bless you. **Humble yourselves therefore under the mighty hand of God, that he may exalt you in due time** (1 Peter 5:6).

Keep on honoring God. Keep on walking in love. Keep on giving your tithes. Keep on paying your bills. Don't try to bless yourself. Keep walking in the things of God, and before long you'll be looking back to see the blessings of God chasing you down. They'll come after you. That's what the Bible says. The Bible says blessings will come upon you and overtake you. (Deut. 28:2)

I like those kinds of blessings. I'm sure you do too! You can't get away from them. Why? Because you know how to deal with pressure. You're able to say "no." You're not trying to keep up with anybody. You're not trying to show off to anybody. You're just walking in love, and letting God have His way.

> **Keep thy foot when thou goest to the house of God, and be more ready to hear, than to give the sacrifice of fools: for they consider not that they do evil.**
>
> **Be not rash with thy mouth, and let not thine heart be hasty to utter any thing before God: for God is in heaven, and thou upon earth: therefore let thy words be few.**
>
> **Ecclesiastes 5:1,2**

This Scripture says, **Be not rash with thy mouth.** In other words, don't be so quick to utter everything that comes into your mind. Here again another scripture tells us to be slow to speak, or you'll find yourself getting into trouble.

Proverbs 10:19 teaches that **in the multitude of words there wanteth not sin: but he that refraineth his lips is wise.** You'll find sin where you find a lot of talking. Before long, because you don't know when to be quiet, you'll find yourself saying something you had no business saying. Before you're able to catch yourself, what you said is already out there, and you're thinking, "I wish I had never said that."

Under pressure, be slow to move, slow to speak, and slow to make decisions. Keep listening to God's sound counsel, and let His blessings overtake you.

5

Choose Life

God is not the one who puts pressure on you. He loves you. You're valuable to Him. He loves you so much, He sent Jesus to die for you. Jesus went to hell for you. Why would God put pressure on you?

It's the enemy, Satan, who puts pressure on us. It's Satan who tries to get us to act contrary to the will and Word of God and to get us to act outside of it. Deuteronomy shows us that very clearly.

> See, I have set before thee this day life and good, and death and evil; in that I command thee this day to love the Lord thy God, to walk in his ways, and to keep his commandments and his statutes and his judgments, that thou mayest live and multiply: and the Lord thy God shall bless thee in the land whither thou goest to possess it.

> But if thine heart turn away, so that thou wilt not hear, but shalt be drawn away, and worship other gods, and serve them; I denounce unto you this day, that ye shall surely perish, and that ye shall not prolong your days upon the land, whither thou passest over Jordan to go to possess it.

> **I call heaven and earth to record this day against you, that I have set before you life and death, blessing and cursing: therefore choose life, that both thou and thy seed may live: that thou mayest love the Lord thy God, and that thou mayest obey his voice, and that thou mayest cleave unto him: for he is thy life, and the length of thy days: that thou mayest dwell in the land which the Lord sware unto thy fathers, to Abraham, to Isaac, and to Jacob, to give them.**
> **Deuteronomy 30:15-20**

Notice that in verse 19 God says, *I've set these things before you — now you choose.* In other words, *I'm not going to pressure you to do anything.*

Many people say, "If God wants me saved, He will get me saved." He's not going to make you get saved! Some people say, "If God wants me filled with the Holy Ghost, He will fill me with the Holy Ghost." He's not going to make you get filled with the Holy Ghost! You choose!

God puts you in the position to find out the truth. Then when you hear the truth, He wants you to make up your mind. If God was going to make us do anything, He would make us all get saved, because He's not willing that anyone should perish. (2 Peter 3:9) He wants everyone to repent. He's not *making* anyone get saved. He's not twisting your arm to go to heaven. He's not making you serve Him. At any time, I can choose to go and live for the devil. At any time, I can choose that, but I've got better sense!

> **For the wages of sin is death; but the gift of God is eternal life through Jesus Christ our Lord.**
> **Romans 6:23**

I can at any time put my Bible down and go out there, get high and try all types of things, but they're going to lead me to destruction. Proverbs 14:12 says:

There is a way which seemeth right unto a man, but the end thereof are the ways of death.

God won't say, "No. I'm not going to let you go out there!" He's not going to do that. He's going to say, "Son, you know how much I love you, and I desire for you to serve Me out of love. I haven't made robots. I've made people — free moral agents who can choose life or choose death."

I had enough sense to know that when I found life, I should stay with it!

Choose Jesus

If you haven't yet met Jesus, you need to ask Him to come into your life. The sin you might find yourself in is sending you to destruction. You know within yourself how miserable you might be or are. All you have to do is choose life.

Choose it! As soon as you choose it, it becomes yours. There's no power in this earth, in hell or in the spirit realm that can keep you from receiving the light of God, if you choose it. That's how powerful your will to choose is. God gave you that will. It's set before you today.

Understand that God doesn't put pressure on us. We're free moral agents. We choose the way we want to go. It's just that it's to our advantage to always choose the ways of God. He's not going to put pressure on us to receive the things He has for us or to walk in His ways. He will just show us how good

He is, how loving He is and how merciful He is. Then He expects us to make our own choice.

God so loved you that He sent His only begotten Son, that if you'll just believe, you'll not perish but you'll have everlasting life. (John 3:16) Choose life today!

6

Turn to God's Answer

As we saw in the first chapter, when some people are under pressure, they look for ways to try to escape from that pressure.

Some people say, ''I've got to get away from it all.'' Some men will spend the whole day at the golf course, and some ladies will spend the whole day at the sewing machine or in the mall.

Some guys go play basketball saying, "I've got to go play. I'm tired of everything. There's too much pressure on me. I need a release!"

But running away is the wrong thing to do! When you are under pressure, escape is the last thing you need. Escape will not help you. Don't turn to some sport or to sewing or to the telephone or to the television. Now don't take me wrong. Those things are fine for relaxation, exercise or other purposes, but not as a way to try to deal with pressure. The answer to pressure is in God's Word. Turn to the Word of God.

Consider Jesus. In Matthew, chapter 4, we'll see an example of Jesus turning to the Scriptures when He was under pressure.

"It is Written"!

Then was Jesus led up of the Spirit into the wilderness to be tempted of the devil. And when he had fasted forty days and forty nights, he was afterward an hungered. And when the tempter came to him, he said, If thou be the Son of God, command that these stones be made bread.

But he (Jesus) answered and said, It is written, Man shall not live by bread alone, but by every word that proceedeth out of the mouth of God.

Then the devil taketh him up into the holy city, and setteth him on a pinnacle of the temple, and saith unto him, If thou be the Son of God, cast thyself down: for it is written, He shall give his angels charge concerning thee: and in their hands they shall bear thee up, lest at any time thou dash thy foot against a stone.

Jesus said unto him, It is written again, Thou shalt not tempt the Lord thy God.

Matthew 4:1-7

Notice how many times Jesus said, "It is written . . . . It is written"! Each time the enemy took a Scripture and put it into Jesus' mind, Jesus countered with "It is written . . . . " He knew the Word of God, and He used it to defeat the tempter.

Jesus knew that the devil was taking Scriptures out of context to try to trick Him into falling for the temptation. Jesus knew what the devil was doing.

The Bible says to compare **spiritual things with spiritual** (1 Cor. 2:13). Don't ever just take a Scripture and go off running with it. Take the time to search out its meaning. Research it. Analyze it. Run references. Know its meaning and in what context it is to be used. Make sure your understanding of that Scripture is consistent throughout the Bible.

> **Again, the devil taketh him up into an exceeding high mountain, and sheweth him all the kingdoms of the world, and the glory of them; and saith unto him, All these things will I give thee, if thou wilt fall down and worship me.**
>
> **Then saith Jesus unto him, Get thee hence, Satan: for it is written, Thou shalt worship the Lord thy God, and him only shalt thou serve.**
>
> **Then the devil leaveth him . . . .**
>
> **Matthew 4:8-11**

When did the devil leave? After Jesus whipped him with the Word. **Then the devil leaveth him, and, behold, angels came and ministered unto him** (Matt. 4:11).

Knowledge of God's Word Is the Key

Knowledge is a key to eliminating pressure.

Let's say that to get a certain job, I have to prove I know how to run a certain machine. If I know how to operate it, if I know all the "ins" and "outs" of it, then there's no pressure on me. Do you know who the pressure is on? It's on the guy who's never operated it, or on the guy who has only operated it a time or two.

But the person who has run that machine all of his life is confident. He's got knowledge. He knows all about that machine. He knows it inside out. He knows what makes it tick, and that gives him confidence. He passes that exam so easily.

Knowledge is a key to eliminating pressure, and Jesus had knowledge. Jesus knew God's Word.

The devil came and applied pressure on Him. Jesus had been fasting for forty days and nights. I don't think that Jesus went into the wilderness to be tempted by the devil. I believe He went there to pray for direction concerning His ministry. I don't think He went there with the intention of allowing the devil to tempt Him for a while. I believe He went to pray and seek the wisdom of God.

Jesus knew His purpose. He came to do the will of Him Who sent Him and to show mankind what God is really like. I believe Jesus was up there to pray because He knew He needed to fellowship with God before He launched into fulfilling that ministry.

After forty days of praying and worshipping God, the enemy came to Him at His weakest point physically. But Jesus was also at His strongest point spiritually.

You can't stay in the presence of God for any length of time without getting strong. You just can't do it. That's why we need to read the Word, meditate it, and pray and fellowship with the Father daily. Don't just spend five minutes — spend some time with Him. It will give you knowledge. It will give you insight. It will give you understanding.

The Bible says we are to meditate on the Word day and night, **for then thou shalt make thy way prosperous, and then thou shalt have good success**

(Josh. 1:8). The Word of God will give you insight, understanding, clarity and wisdom. It will strengthen you.

Jesus was strong spiritually. But His flesh must have been getting weak. You can't fast for any length of time without getting weak physically. The Bible says, **he was afterward an hungred** (Matt. 4:2). He was hungry.

The human body will go for a length of time, living off the fat and energies that have already been stored up. Then, after a while, the body begins to say, ''If I don't get food right now, I can't go on.'' Jesus had reached the point where He needed food. His body was automatically saying, ''You're hungry. You have to eat.''

When you enter a fast, after a while you don't get hungry. After the first few days, hunger just totally leaves you. Your body is now living off the energies of stored food and fat. But after a certain amount of time, you have to eat. Your body will demand it, and Jesus had reached that point. His body demanded it.

That's the moment Satan chose to come and say, ''Now if You be the Son of God . . . .''

''If . . . if . . . if . . . .'' The devil will always question the things of God with ''if . . . .'' The devil was there when Jesus was baptized by John the Baptist. The devil heard God's voice from heaven, saying, **This is my beloved Son, in whom I am well pleased** (Matt. 3:17). He was there to observe the Holy Spirit descending upon Jesus like a dove. He knew Jesus was the Son of God, and he was saying, ''*If* . . . .'' ''*If* You

are the Son of God, turn this stone into bread . . . .''
''*If* You are the Son of God, cast yourself down. . .'' *If!*

But Jesus knew the Word; He had knowledge. In the midst of pressure, He did not give in to the devil. He turned to the Word. He said, **It is written, Man shall not live by bread alone, but by every word that proceedeth out of the mouth of God.**

The Word of God
Will Put You Over

The Word of God is what will cause you to win. Jesus knew that. He used the Word, and He used the Word, and He used the Word, until finally the devil said, ''I've got to get out of here! This man won't budge!''

Did you know that you can stay in the Word long enough until you won't budge? No matter how strong the pressure is, no matter how bad it seems, you will be so full of the Word of God that you won't budge.

You'll say, ''*The Word of God says . . . .* '' and ''*I'm not moved by what I feel and what I see and what I think.*''

The devil sees that courage, that boldness, that confidence, that assurance, and he will leave. And if God sent His angels to minister to Jesus, He will send angels to minister to us.

Turn to the Word in the midst of pressure. And that will get your mind thinking thoughts of God. When you have knowledge of the Word of God, you can win over anything.

> **I beseech you therefore, brethren, by the mercies of God, that ye present your bodies a living sacrifice, holy, acceptable unto God, which is your reasonable service.**

> **And be not conformed to this world: but be ye transformed by the renewing of your mind, that ye may prove what is that good, and acceptable, and perfect, will of God.**
>
> **Romans 12:1,2**

God says not to be conformed to this world, **but be ye transformed by the renewing of your mind.**

Under pressure, the enemy will always try to get you to do things the way the world does them. When the pressure comes, the enemy will always say, "Why don't you do this?" or "Why don't you do that?" He will always come up with natural concepts, alternatives and reasonings. And if it isn't the enemy bringing those thoughts to you, then it is your own body, your own flesh, your own mind beginning to think that way: *"Well, make it easy for yourself . . . ."*

Instead of turning to television, the phone, magazines or recreation, turn to the Word of God. Turn to the Word and begin to study, to meditate. Or simply turn to God and pray:

"Father, I need to look up some things concerning this situation. Give me some insight. I know Your Word has an exceeding great and precious promise for everything."

That's what Second Peter 1:4 says:

> **Whereby are given unto us exceeding great and precious promises: that by these ye might be partakers of the divine nature, having escaped the corruption that is in the world through lust.**

Pray:

"Father, the pressure has come. I thank You for my victory because You have overcome the world. I refuse to walk by the dictates of the flesh, but rather by the Word of God. Father, what do You have to say about this? I believe I receive Your help!"

Begin to look up scriptures concerning what you are going through, and the Lord will begin to give you His mind and His way of looking at the situation. And the Word will begin to renew your mind. It will strengthen you and it will cause you to win, because it will cause you to walk like Jesus walked.

The Word will cause you to rise up on the inside and speak to that mountain and say, "**Remove hence** (Matt. 17:20) for it is written . . . . "

The Word of God is what gives us the victory — the Word and only the Word.

We need to remember that Jesus used the Word of God to deal with the pressure Satan brought against Him in the wilderness. He kept on saying, "It is written . . . . it is written . . . . it is written." He had the Word inside Him.

> **Grace and peace be multiplied unto you through the knowledge of God, and of Jesus our Lord, according as his divine power hath given unto us all things that pertain unto life and godliness, through the knowledge of him that hath called us to glory and virtue:**
>
> **Whereby are given unto us exceeding great and precious promises: that by these ye might be partakers of the divine nature, having escaped the corruption that is in the world through lust.**
>
> **2 Peter 1:2-4**

How do we get the things that pertain to life and godliness? Through the *knowledge* of Him that has called us to glory and virtue. It doesn't matter what your challenge is.

Peter is telling us in these verses that by the Word of God, we can escape. We can overcome. It doesn't matter what your seemingly unique challenge is, or how impossible it seems. We can rule over all the things to which the enemy has caused man to be enslaved. We can overcome through the exceeding great and precious promises. But we're never going to learn what those promises are if we don't spend time in the Word.

God has a way of doing things, and the world has a way of doing things. The world automatically says when you're broke, go borrow. God says when you're broke or don't have anything, give something. By doing things God's way, you'll be able to escape the pressure. You'll be able to overcome. You'll be able to win. But you can't do that when you're not spending time in the Word.

We have to spend time meditating, feeding our spirit man with the Word of God, renewing our minds so that we won't automatically and immediately go the way of the world.

As we saw before, everybody deals with pressure: little children, young adults, elderly people. But if you use the Word of God long enough on the devil, he will leave you. If you don't use it, Satan will stay right there with you. Know the Word of God. Speak it and act on it!

7

Overcome Pressure
Through Prayer

When we are faced with pressure, I believe it's absolutely vital for us to pray. It's important to get before God. Turn to the Word to find out what God says about your current situation, then pray. Pray the Word. Pray the answer. Don't pray the problem. The Word of God is the answer. Confess the Word over your situation.

The better we are at handling pressure, the more valuable we are to the Kingdom of God. God wants people who are bold and courageous and ready to go after the situation.

The Bible says that God spoke to Gideon when his men were getting ready to go to war. (Judg. 7:2-7.)

God said, ''Gideon, you have over 20,000 men. That's too many. What I want you to do is stand up before the people and say to them, 'All of you who are afraid, go home.' ''

One by one, the men who were afraid began to leave. But in God's eyes, there were still too many men.

God said, "I'll tell you what to do. Go down to this brook over here, and just observe the way the men drink the water. The ones who drink a certain way, those are the ones you use."

Finally out of 20,000 men, only 300 were left. They were greatly outnumbered. That's pressure! But they weren't ready to run. They were ready to tackle the enemy! Those 300 men were fit for the task. They were bold. They were courageous. They were ready to deal with pressure and take on the situation. They were ready! They were good at handling pressure, and they were more valuable to the Kingdom of God than thousands of men.

Don't Let Trivial Things Set You Back

Jeremiah 12:5 says, **If thou hast run with the footmen, and they have wearied thee, then how canst thou contend with horses?** If the footmen are getting to you, then what will you do when the men on horses come your way?

If the little problems of life get to you and set you back, and you murmur, complain and cry out, "Why me, God?" what will happen when the enemy makes up his mind to come in on you like a flood? What then? If the trivial things of life set you back, what will happen if Satan says, "All you demons, go after him!"

All the devil has to do to some Christians is the same thing over and over again, just present the same situation to them time after time, and they lose their cool. They fly off the handle: "Why me, God? I'm tired of it! I've had it with that!" Well, what's going to happen when the men on horses come in?

If you are a man or woman of prayer, you'll be ready. You'll have been in the Word. You'll have been before the Father in prayer. You'll put your shoulders back. You'll put your head up. You'll say, *"You may come in like a flood, Satan, but the Spirit of the Lord raises up a standard against you, and the gates of hell shall not prevail against me!"* You'll say, *"Hey — I win! I'm more than a conqueror!"* (Is. 59:19, Matt. 16:18, Rom. 8:37)

Pray

Sometimes an attack from the enemy will be so light, you'll hardly even feel it. Because you're able to deal with that, you'll take that in stride. But every now and then, the enemy will increase his attacks against you. He will increase the pressure, more and more. And if minor things set you back, when the attack increases, you're not going to make it. You'll fall on your face.

God wants us to be able to overcome anything that the enemy brings against us. Anything — no matter if it's minor or major. Whether it's small or great. He wants us to be able to overcome it. Prayer is the key to overcoming.

Look at the example of Jesus' life.

> **And forthwith, when they were come out of the synagogue, they entered into the house of Simon and Andrew, with James and John. But Simon's wife's mother lay sick of a fever, and anon they tell him of her.**

And he came and took her by the hand, and lifted her up; and immediately the fever left her, and she ministered unto them. And at even, when the sun did set, they brought unto him all that were diseased, and them that were possessed with devils. And all the city was gathered together at the door.

And he healed many that were sick of divers diseases, and cast out many devils; and suffered not the devils to speak, because they knew him.

And in the morning, rising up a great while before day, he went out, and departed into a solitary place, and there prayed.

And Simon and they that were with him followed after him. And when they had found him, they said unto him, All men seek for thee.

Mark 1:29-37

Get this picture: Sometime during the day, Jesus entered into Simon Peter's house and healed his mother-in-law. By evening, a great multitude had gathered at the door. Jesus went out among them and began to cast out devils and heal the sick. The blind received their sight. The deaf received their hearing. The dumb began to speak. I would imagine that His physical body was worn down.

People were always trying to get to Him. When people are always trying to draw something from you, always wanting to talk to you, always demanding something of you; when all men want to understand God and believe you have the answer; when they always expect something from you and you always have to produce, tell me that doesn't create pressure! Mothers, fathers, employers and supervisors have some idea of what I mean. Jesus had to have been presented with pressure, and, physically, He had to have been tired.

And what did He do? After Jesus finished ministering to all those people, verse 35 says He rose up a great while before day and went to a solitary place and prayed. He was probably thinking: *I've got to pray! There's so much that people are expecting from Me and drawing out of Me; the pressure is so great, I need to get up and pray. I've got to pray more than I've been praying. I've got to talk to My Father a little bit more. I need to commune with Him, get built up, and maintain My peace and inner strength.*

So He got up to pray while the other people were still sleeping.

> . . . he went out, and departed into a solitary place, and there prayed. And Simon and they that were with him followed after him. And when they had found him, they said unto him, All men seek for thee.
>
> **Mark 1:35-37**

Again people sought Him! All men were seeking for Him; all men wanted Him to touch them; all men wanted Him to talk to them; all men wanted Him to answer their questions. The way Jesus dealt with that kind of demanding pressure was to pray.

When the pressure comes, you've got to pray to overcome it. Sometimes the pressure can get so great that the fifteen minutes or the half hour you normally pray isn't enough — it won't get you over. Sometimes you need to set the alarm clock a little bit earlier to get up and pray and spend more time with the Father.

Yes — be still; be slow to move. Yes — go to the Word of God. But also pray.

Jesus Knew All About Pressure

And it came to pass also on another sabbath, that he entered into the synagogue and taught: and there was a man whose right hand was withered. And the scribes and Pharisees watched him, whether he would heal on the sabbath day; that they might find an accusation against him.

But he knew their thoughts, and said to the man which had the withered hand, Rise up, and stand forth in the midst. And he arose and stood forth. Then said Jesus unto them, I will ask you one thing; Is it lawful on the sabbath days to do good, or to do evil? to save life, or to destroy it?

And looking round about upon them all, he said unto the man, Stretch forth thy hand. And he did so: and his hand was restored whole as the other.

And they were filled with madness; and communed one with another what they might do to Jesus.

Luke 6:6-11

Not being able to move without someone watching you — that's pressure. You may know exactly what I'm talking about if on your job, there's a supervisor looking over your shoulder to see if you're slothful. You know the supervisor is watching to see if you're really producing, and that creates pressure. Some people can't handle it. Some people go home every night and say, "I'm going to quit that job. I can't take it anymore!"

If that happens to you, get before God and pray.

Jesus knew the scribes and Pharisees were watching Him. He knew their thoughts. But He healed the man's withered hand anyway. The scribes and Pharisees were filled with madness! They were upset — angry, full of rage; they were out to kill Jesus and destroy His ministry. They talked among themselves: "What are we going to do with this man called Jesus? He knows it's the Sabbath day, and He went ahead and healed that man anyway!"

The scribes and the Pharisees were plotting, planning and conniving, but Jesus knew what was going on. And how did He deal with the pressure?

> **And it came to pass in those days, that he went out into a mountain to pray, and continued all night in prayer to God.**
>
> **Luke 6:12**

Jesus doubled up on His prayer time. Instead of rising early, He spent all night in prayer.

How do you react when you find out other people have been talking about you? Some people react by writing the other people off. They don't want to talk to them anymore. Other people are ready to put on boxing gloves. Those are signs of not being able to deal with pressure.

When the pressure gets to the point that you're saying, "I don't know what to do! I don't know how I'm going to handle this!" double up on your prayer time. Pray more than you've ever prayed. If you have to pray all night, stay up all night praying and fellowshipping with God, getting built up on the inside. The key to overcoming that pressure is prayer!

8

When You Don't Know
How To Pray

Sometimes the pressure coming against you can be so great that a mental prayer just isn't enough. A "mental prayer" just comes out of your head. It's based on your vocabulary, your education, or maybe even on how your mother or your father taught you to pray.

Sometimes the pressure gets so strong, you don't know how to talk to God out of your head, in English, I mean. You don't know how to express yourself. You don't know how to form the right words based on your education. And praying what we call the Lord's Prayer, **Our Father which art in heaven, Hallowed be Thy name** . . . , won't get you over.

If you're not able to pray out of your spirit and bypass your brain — bypass what you're thinking — by praying in another language, you are limiting your ability to win as quickly as possible.

When you're faced with the kind of pressure that's trying to wipe you out, steal your joy, steal your finances and break up your home, you'll need to be able to pray out of your spirit. To do that you'll need to be filled with the Holy Spirit — the Holy Ghost.

"Filled with the Holy Ghost," you may say. "What's that?"

> And when the day of Pentecost was fully come, they were all with one accord in one place. And suddenly there came a sound from heaven as of a rushing mighty wind, and it filled all the house where they were sitting. And there appeared unto them cloven tongues like as of fire, and it sat upon each of them.
>
> And they were all filled with the Holy Ghost, and began to speak with other tongues, as the Spirit gave them utterance.
>
> Acts 2:1-4

The Bible says that when they were filled with the Holy Ghost, they began to speak with other tongues as the Spirit gave them utterance.

You may say, "Filled with the Holy Ghost? I thought I got it all when Jesus came into my life."

That's not what the Bible teaches. You don't receive the *fullness* of the gift of the Holy Spirit, the power of God, the ability to pray in other tongues, when you receive Jesus in your life. This happens separately.

> In the last day, that great day of the feast, Jesus stood and cried, saying, If any man thirst, let him come unto me, and drink. He that believeth on me, as the scripture hath said, out of his belly shall flow rivers of living water.

(But this spake he of the Spirit, which they
that believe on him should receive: for the Holy
Ghost was not yet given; because that Jesus was
not yet glorified.)

John 7:37-39

Look at the boldness of Jesus! He proclaimed this
to the guests at the feast. In the midst of their traditions
and traditional thinking, Jesus just stood up and said,
If any man thirst, let him come unto me, and drink.
(Jesus is the answer!)

Notice that it says, **they that believe on him
should receive.** Your receiving is to take place after
your believing. Then *out of my belly will flow rivers of
living water.* This means that you will begin to speak
in a heavenly language as they did on the Day of
Pentecost.

The Samaritans Needed More

Then Philip went down to the city of Samaria,
and preached Christ unto them. And the people with
one accord gave heed unto those things which Philip
spake, hearing and seeing the miracles which he did.

For unclean spirits, crying with loud voice, came
out of many that were possessed with them: and many
taken with palsies, and that were lame, were healed.
And there was great joy in that city.

Acts 8:5-8

Philip preached Christ. He preached that Jesus
became sin for us, that He died and went into hell, was
resurrected and then He ascended to the Father. And
the Samaritans believed the Word that Philip preached.

When you really preach Christ, there will be signs
following. There were signs and wonders following,
and great joy was in that city.

Word reached Jerusalem that the people of Samaria had received the Word of God. (In other words, they received Christ — they believed the Word that Philip preached.) When the apostles in Jerusalem heard this, they sent Peter and John.

> **Now when the apostles which were at Jerusalem heard that Samaria had received the word of God, they sent unto them Peter and John: who, when they were come down, prayed for them, that they might receive the Holy Ghost:**
>
> **(For as yet he was fallen upon none of them: only they were baptized in the name of the Lord Jesus.)**
>
> **Then laid they their hands on them, and they received the Holy Ghost.**
>
> **Acts 8:14-17**

We just saw that the people in Samaria believed the Word of God; they believed on Christ. Then verse 16 tells us that they were already baptized in Christ when Peter and John came. But the Holy Ghost hadn't come on them yet. The only thing the people of Samaria could do was to pray out of their heads. They needed more than that; they needed to pray in the Spirit.

Peter and John laid their hands on the Samaritans, and they received the Holy Ghost. Out of their bellies began to flow rivers of living water. They began to pray in other tongues in the same way the 120 did on the Day of Pentecost. (Acts 1:15)

The Spirit of God
Will Give You Utterance

In Ephesians 6:18, Paul tells us of the importance of praying in the Spirit. (In the second part of the verse, Paul was exhorting the believers to pray in the Spirit.)

> **Praying always with all prayer and supplication in the Spirit, and watching thereunto with all perseverance and supplication for all saints.**

Pray "in the Spirit."

John 4:24 says:

> **God is a** *Spirit:* **and they that worship him must worship him** *in spirit* **and in truth.**

Acts 2:4 tells us:

> **And they were all filled with the Holy Ghost, and began to speak with other tongues, as** *the Spirit* **gave them utterance.**

If you pray out of your head, based on your vocabulary, that can't be praying in the Spirit. That type of praying is praying out of your understanding. Then how do you pray in the Spirit?

You pray in the Spirit by being filled with the Holy Ghost; then, as an act of your will, you release your faith, begin to open up your mouth in faith, and the Spirit of God, as He did on the Day of Pentecost, will give you utterance. You'll begin to speak in a heavenly language to the Father of spirits.

Talk to God
Spirit to Spirit

From the Day of Pentecost on — when **they were all filled with the Holy Ghost, and began to speak with other tongues** (Acts 2:4), they were able to pray to God two ways — mentally and spiritually.

As we just saw, John 4:24 says,

> **God is a Spirit: and they that worship him must worship him in spirit and in truth.**

Hebrews 12:9 says God is the **Father of spirits.**

Whether or not you realize it, you are a spirit. You are a spirit being. You have a soul. And you live in a body. And being a spirit being, created in God's image, in the class of God, you need to be able to talk to God out of your spirit — spirit to Spirit.

Yes, God understands our mental prayers, but it's good to be able to talk to Him spirit to Spirit. Every born-again child of God needs to talk to Him that way.

> **Follow after charity, and desire spiritual gifts, but rather that ye may prophesy. For he that speaketh in an unknown tongue speaketh not unto men, but unto God: for no man understandeth him; howbeit in the spirit he speaketh mysteries.**
>
> **1 Corinthians 14:1,2**

Notice that when you speak in an unknown tongue, you speak to God. You're not talking to man. You're talking to God, and God — your Father — understands you. Notice that this scripture states that you are *speaking mysteries.*

Every time I pray out of my head in English, the devil hears and understands it. But when I go over into my prayer language and pray in the Spirit, the devil can't tap into that. He can't break the code! Only God the Father understands my heavenly language. I like that! I love that!

When pressure comes my way, I don't need to blurt out everything that comes into my mind. I need to start praying in tongues and pray out of my spirit to my Father, then I'll be speaking mysteries that only my Father God can understand. The beauty of it is in those pressurized situations, the Holy Ghost helps me to pray according to the mind or will of God. (Rom. 8:26,27; 1 Cor. 2:10-12)

Build Yourself Up

When you're under pressure, you need to stay built up, charged up. Studying the Word of God will do that. But also, Jude 20 tells us that praying in the Spirit will do that:

> But ye, beloved, building up yourselves on your most holy faith, praying in the Holy Ghost.

First Corinthians 14:3,4:

> But he that prophesieth speaketh unto men to edification, and exhortation, and comfort. He that speaketh in an unknown tongue edifieth himself....

He **edifieth** himself. That means he charges himself up; he builds himself up.

Have you ever gone outside in the winter time, when the temperature happens to be 18 degrees? There you are, ready to go to work, and you step into your automobile and say, "Come on, Betsy — just crank on up this morning!"

You get the key and stick it into the ignition. But before you even turn it, you put your foot on that accelerator, trying to get that gas on up there, because you want that car to start. After you wait a couple of seconds, you turn the key. Then you wait.

The first thing that hits you is, "It's not going to start!" Your next thought is, "I've flooded it!"

You wait and you wait. Finally, you decide the battery needs charging. And if you have another automobile, you tell your spouse, "Come on out — get the other car. Get the cables. My battery needs to be charged!"

If you don't have another automobile, then you go next door: "Come on — I need my car jumped!"

You call a neighbor; you call *somebody!* You know your battery needs charging, and you have to get to work.

Your neighbor comes and connects the jumper cables to the battery posts. He gets in his car and lets it run a little bit first, just to boost up the energy. Then you get in your car and turn the key. It cranks right up. What happened? The battery got charged.

The Bible teaches us that when we pray in the Holy Ghost — pray in the Spirit — our spirit man is charged and built up (the same way a car battery is built up). And in the midst of pressure, we need to pray not only in our English language, but also in tongues. We need to pray in tongues and build up our spirit man so we won't lie down.

Jesus asked one man, **Wilt thou be made whole?** (John 5:6). That man was lying down on the inside. A lot of Christians are lying down on the inside. Why? Because they don't know how to build themselves up. They don't know how to charge themselves up. All you have to do is be filled with the Spirit and pray in the Holy Ghost.

In Acts, chapter 10, Peter — a Jew — went to the house of Cornelius — a Gentile — to preach Jesus. As he preached, they received the Holy Ghost. When Peter got back to Jerusalem, he was called on the carpet.

"Why did you go over there?" the other apostles asked.

Peter said, "God appeared to me and I had to go. And as I was preaching, they received the Holy Ghost the same way we did — they began to speak with other tongues."

Every time people received the Holy Ghost in the Bible, they began to speak with other tongues. This meant they could edify themselves or build themselves up. When you're under pressure, you have to be able to do that.

Sometimes just words from your friends are not enough. Most of them will say, "Just hang in there!" But the Bible doesn't tell us to *hang*. It tells us to *stand!*

I don't want to *hang*. I want to *stand!* Ephesians 6:13 says, "Having done all, stand . . . ."

When the pressure gets so great that you don't know how to express yourself in the English language, if you're not built up, you'll lie down. If you lie down, that means you've fainted in your mind, and if you've fainted in your mind, you've lost. Stay built up; pray in the Spirit.

Be Filled
With the Holy Spirit!

God wants you to have the infilling of the Holy Ghost today. He wants you to be able to talk to Him out of your spirit, because God is a Spirit and He wants spirit communicating with Spirit. He's the Father of spirits.

If you haven't been filled with the Holy Spirit, you can be filled right now. You don't have to wait. Just ask the Father.

> **And I say unto you, Ask, and it shall be given you; seek, and ye shall find; knock, and it shall be opened unto you. For every one that asketh receiveth; and he that seeketh findeth; and to him that knocketh it shall be opened.**

> If a son shall ask bread of any of you that is a father, will he give him a stone? or if he ask a fish, will he for a fish give him a serpent? or if he shall ask an egg, will he offer him a scorpion?
>
> If ye then, being evil, know how to give good gifts unto your children: *how much more shall your heavenly Father give the Holy Spirit to them that ask him?*
>
> **Luke 11:9-13**

I *love* those positive words! No doubt about it: you *shall* find. It *shall* be given. Knock and it *shall* be opened unto you. For *everyone* that asketh receiveth!

It doesn't matter how rotten a life a man has lived, when Christmas time comes, he wants to give his children some gifts. No matter how rotten he's been all year long or how many times he's been considered a bad father — no matter if he's lived a life of a drunkard or if he's been living out in the world, when Christmas time comes, he wants to do something good for his children. He wants to give them good gifts.

Verse 13: **How much more shall your heavenly Father give the Holy Spirit to them that ask him?**

All you have to do is ask! And when you ask, God is going to give you *exactly* what you ask for. If you ask for the infilling of the Holy Spirit, you'll get it.

You might say, "How will I know if it's the real thing?"

You'll know because God said it!

You might say, "I thought it was of the devil!"

There's nothing bad in God, and nothing good in the devil, and the Holy Ghost comes from God.

If you're born again, simply ask the Father to give you the Holy Spirit. If you're not born again, there is a simple prayer at the end of this book for you to pray to receive the gift of salvation. If you're already born again — if you've already made Jesus your Lord and Savior — then you're ready to receive the Holy Spirit.

Just say, "Father, I ask You right now to fill me with the Holy Ghost." (Pray out loud the prayer at the end of the book to receive the infilling of the Holy Spirit.) And I'm telling you — if you ask in faith, Jesus Himself will take the Holy Ghost and baptize your spirit. And when He gets through with you, you'll be praying in another language, bypassing your mind, talking to the Father, spirit to Spirit.

How do you deal with pressure? Prayer! But to deal with the pressure that the enemy and life and circumstances bring upon us, mental praying is not always enough. You need to be able to pray in the Holy Spirit.

When you get under pressure, pray in the Holy Ghost.*

---

*For further insight or study, I recommend the books: *Why Tongues* by Kenneth E. Hagin (Tulsa: RHEMA Bible Church, 1975) and *The Holy Spirit — The Missing Ingredient* by Frederick K.C. Price (Tulsa: Harrison House, 1978).

Conclusion

Acts, chapter 4, shows us how the apostles reacted when the Pharisees threatened them and warned, "Don't preach anymore in the name of Jesus!"

Faced with that threat, did they say, "Oh, God — what are we going to do now?"

No! They went back to their company, their own church, reported what had happened, then began to pray and praise God. And after they had prayed, they spoke the Word with boldness and gave witness with great power of the resurrection of the Lord Jesus. (verses 31,33) God brought them through the pressure victoriously! And that's what God wants for us — to go from pressure to praise!

When pressure tries to come against you, consider Jesus. Consider the pressure He was under; consider His example, so that you won't faint in your mind. Cast down imaginations, reasoning.

Remember that knowledge of God's Word is a key to eliminating pressure. Think God's thoughts. Meditate on His Word day and night. Be transformed by the renewing of your mind.

Evaluate the situation. Be swift to hear, slow to move, slow to speak. Don't make decisions under pressure. Trust in the Lord with all your heart rather than leaning to your own understanding. In all your ways acknowledge Him, and He will direct your paths. Be still and know that He is God. Let the Holy Spirit give you guidance in your circumstances.

Remember that God is not the source of pressure. Choose God's way — choose life.

When Jesus was under pressure, He prayed. When the disciples were under pressure, they prayed. When we're under pressure, we need to pray. Once we've found what the Word says about the situation facing us right now, we need to pray it, confess it and act on it. And when the pressure is so bad that we don't know how to pray in English, we can pray in the Holy Spirit. But before that, we'll pray in the Spirit to edify ourselves, to build ourselves up and to charge ourselves up so that we won't just "hang in there," we'll *stand*!

We don't have to choke under pressure. We can have victory over pressure. And God promises victory!

Thanks be to God, which giveth us the victory through our Lord Jesus Christ!

1 Corinthians 15:57

Prayers

Prayer for Salvation

Dear God, I am a sinner. I need a Savior. I need Jesus. I ask Jesus now to come into my life. I believe in my heart that You raised Jesus from the dead, and I confess Him as Lord.

Thank You for coming into my life and forgiving me of sins. I call myself a child of God. In Jesus' name. Amen.

Prayer To Receive
the Infilling of the Holy Spirit

Father, You promise that if I seek You, I will find You. Your Word says that You will give me the Holy Spirit if I ask You. I'm coming to You in faith, asking You to fill me with Your Holy Spirit. I receive the Holy Spirit now, by faith, in Jesus' name. I yield my tongue to You now, believing that You will give me my heavenly language so that You and I can communicate, spirit to Spirit.

Thank You, Father, for filling me with the Holy Spirit. In Jesus' name.

ROBYN GOOL an outstanding teacher, speaker and writer, is founder and pastor of Victory Christian Center in Charlotte, North Carolina.

Robyn graduated from Oral Roberts University. It was there that he received the gift of the Holy Spirit, met his beautiful and talented wife, Marilyn, and was called by God into ministry.

In 1995 Robyn Gool was given an Honorary Doctorate Degree from Indiana Christian University where the late Dr. Lester Sumrall was president.

With the leadership of this man anointed by God with the heart of a pastor, Victory Christian Center has grown and flourished. The outreach ministry, More Than Conquerors Ministries, includes four radio stations and a community television station (WGTB TV-28). Besides being viewed on WGTB, the More

Than Conquerors Telecast is seen in Charlotte and surrounding areas daily on various stations. A current listing of stations and times is available on the church website — www.vccenter.net. In addition, the ministry operates Conquerors Publishing, which produces More Than Conquerors magazine.

VCC's educational department provides Christian schools for students in K-3 through 12th grade. Its More Than Conquerors College offers degrees and certifications in continuing education, biblical studies and vocational programs.

Church in the City, its inner city ministry founded in 1998, offers hope and positive change for residents of high-risk communities. Last year, VCC expanded this outreach to include a full-service women's shelter.

Other books by Robyn Gool include "Proper Attitudes Toward Leadership," "For Singles Only," "Don't Block the Blessings," "Every Ministry Needs Help" and "What to Do When You're Backed Against the Wall."

Other Books by Robyn Gool

For additional copies of
Pressure to Praise and other books
contact:

The VCC Wordshop
P.O. Box 240433
Charlotte, NC 28224
(704) 602-6011
9:00 AM - 4:45 PM
Monday - Friday

To contact the author, please write:

Pastor Robyn Gool
Victory Christian Center
P.O. Box 240433
Charlotte, NC 28224

*Please include your prayer requests
and comments.*

Conquerors Publishing Vision

Spreading the gospel of Christ to win the lost;
Demonstrating God's never-ending love
and compassion for mankind;
Empowering the Body of Christ to live
victoriously by applying God's Word.